TAYLOR SWIFT

HER STORY

By Lexi Ryals & Grace Mack
Illustrated by Erwin Madrid

Scholastic Inc.

No matter what happens in life, be good to people. Being good to people is a wonderful legacy to leave behind.

—T.S.
(Taylor Swift)

Photo Credits:
Photos ©: cover: Casey Flanigan/imageSPACE/Shutterstock; back cover: AP Photo/Natacha Pisarenko; 2: John Shearer/TAS23/Getty Images for TAS Rights Management; 10-11: photo by TheFunTimesGuide.com; 14: Al Messerschmidt/Getty Images; 15 background: Gino's Premium Images/Alamy Stock Photo; 17: AP Photo/Nati Harnik; 19: Frank Micelotta/Invision/AP Images; 21 center: Al Pereira/WireImage/Getty Images; 21 bottom: Marc Piasecki/FilmMagic/Getty Images; 24: Matt Sayles/Invision/AP; 26 top: Matt Winkelmeyer/TAS18/Getty Images for TAS; 26 center: Patti McConville/Alamy Stock Photo; 27: Gareth Cattermole/TAS18/Getty Images for TAS; 28 center: PjrStudio/Alamy Stock Photo; 28 bottom: PA Images/Alamy Stock Photo; 29: PA Images/Alamy Stock Photo; 30: Stephen Chung/Alamy Stock Photo; 31: Kevin Mazur/Getty Images for The Recording Academy; 32: Matt Winkelmeyer/Getty Images for dcp; 33: Hazel Plater/Alamy Stock Photo; 34 top left, 34 top right, 34 center: Kevin Mazur/Getty Images for TAS Rights Management; 35 center: TAS2023 via Getty Images; 35 bottom: Allen J. Schaben/Los Angeles Times via Getty Images; 36: Allen J. Schaben/Los Angeles Times via Getty Images; 37 top: John Shearer/Getty Images for TAS; 38: AP Photo/Evan Agostini; 39 center: New Line/Kobal/Shutterstock; 39 bottom: Universal Pictures/Moviestore/Shutterstock; 40 top right: Kevork Djansezian/Getty Images; 40 center: Denise Truscello/WireImage/Getty Images; 41: AP Photo/George Walker IV; 42: Kevin Mazur/Getty Images; 43: PacificCoastNews/Newscom; 44: Jeff Kravitz/FilmMagic/Getty Images; 45: John Shearer/Getty Images for TAS Rights Management. All other stock photos © Getty Images and Shutterstock.com.

This unauthorized biography was carefully researched to make sure it's accurate. Although the book is written to sound like Taylor Swift speaking to the reader, these are not her actual statements. Portions of this book were previously published under the title *When I Grow Up: Taylor Swift*.

Text and illustrations © 2015, 2024 by Scholastic Inc.

ISBN 978-1-5461-4274-4

10 9 8 7 6 5 4 3 2 1   24 25 26 27 28

Printed in the U.S.A.   40
First printing, August 2024

Book design by Cheung Tai

DAD

MOM

AUSTIN

ME

My name is Taylor Swift. I was born on December 13, 1989, in Reading, Pennsylvania. I grew up in a small town nearby, called Wyomissing, on a Christmas tree farm with my parents and my younger brother, Austin. My mom ran the farm and my dad worked for a financial company.

I've known I wanted to be a country music star since I was around ten years old, when I got my first country music **album**, *Blue*, by LeAnn Rimes. I listened to it over and over until I had memorized every song. My parents encouraged my dream by enrolling me in singing lessons.

(A) nother dream of mine was to perform onstage, so my parents signed me up for acting lessons, too. I starred as Sandy in a local production of the musical *Grease*. I also auditioned for different Broadway shows in New York City, which was only a bus ride away from my hometown. But I never got any of the parts I auditioned for.

Back home, I began to focus more on music. I started singing **karaoke** at local fairs and festivals when I was ten years old. I won several contests and even got to open a hometown show for the Charlie Daniels Band, country music legends.

When I was eleven, I recorded my first **demo tape** of me singing my favorite country songs. My mom drove me down to Nashville, Tennessee, where many country music stars get their start, and I left my demo with all of the country **music labels**. Unfortunately, no one wanted to give me a **record deal** then. But I wasn't about to give up on my dream!

In sixth grade, my friends decided they didn't like me anymore. They left me out of the group and made fun of me. It was awful! I learned to play guitar that year and started writing songs. I always turned to music when I felt sad, and it made me feel better to write down how I was feeling. I wrote one of my very first songs about those mean girls. It's called "The Outside."

"THE OUTSIDE"

So how can I ever try to be better? Nobody ever lets me in

My family could see how serious I was about becoming a country music singer. I spent nearly all my time writing songs, singing, practicing guitar, and performing whenever I could. When a music label offered me a **development deal**, my whole family moved with me to Nashville. They've always supported my music dreams!

Unfortunately, my development deal didn't work out. That company wasn't interested in letting me write my own songs, so I knew it wasn't a good fit. I was disappointed, but it only made me more determined to write great songs and find the right music label to work with.

I kept writing songs, and when I was fourteen, Sony offered me a job as a staff writer. I was the youngest writer they'd ever had! I worked with more experienced songwriters who helped me learn how to really express myself.

When I was sixteen, I finally signed a record deal, with Big Machine Records. I was so excited! Big Machine Records brought in some of the best **producers** in country music to help me record my first album, *Taylor Swift*. They gave me lots of guidance, but they also listened to what I wanted. Recording in a professional music studio was really fun, but it was also a ton of work to juggle with high school!

A lot of people didn't think a teenager should record an album. They said that no one would want to listen to songs about teenage problems. But my record label believed in me. Since I'd been writing songs for three years, I had a lot of material to choose from! I'd written about my ex-friends, my first boyfriend, and having a crush on a boy who didn't know I liked him. My music came from my heart, and the feelings I sang about were familiar to other teens like me.

Luckily, lots of people (and not just teens) loved my music! Within a year, *Taylor Swift* went **platinum**. My first hit was "Tim McGraw," followed by "Teardrops on My Guitar." I got to go on tour as the opening act for different country music stars, including George Strait and Rascal Flatts. It was tough to balance music, high school, and friends, but it was worth it. I graduated with great grades, and I loved being on the road and getting to meet all my new fans.

I couldn't wait to record another album. My second album, *Fearless*, came out in 2008, when I was eighteen years old. I worked with other songwriters and producers, but I wrote most of the songs myself. Two of the most popular songs from *Fearless* were "Love Story" and "You Belong With Me." The album went platinum almost immediately—it was so cool! I went on a yearlong tour that took me all over the United States. It was my first time **headlining** a tour, and I had so much fun! I couldn't believe that my dreams of being a country music star were all coming true.

My third album, *Speak Now*, came out in 2010, when I was twenty-two years old. It debuted at number one and has sold more than 6 million copies! This was the first time I'd written every song on an album all by myself, so it meant a lot to me. As usual, I wrote songs about things that had actually happened in my life, including "Back to December," which was an apology to an ex-boyfriend, and "Mean," which was my way of telling a music critic to stop bullying me.

I went on my *Speak Now* world tour for almost two years, playing huge arenas around the globe. I'd never had the opportunity to travel to so many amazing places. It was exhausting, but so much fun. Luckily, I was able to take breaks between different parts of the tour so that I could rest, spend time with friends and family, and get back into the recording studio to work on my next album.

*R*ed was my fourth album, and it was all about love. I'd had my heart broken a few times by then, so I used those experiences to write many of the songs, like "I Knew You Were Trouble" and "We Are Never Ever Getting Back Together." I worked with songwriters who focused on pop and alternative styles, so it had less of a country sound than my earlier albums. *Red* debuted at number one in October 2012 and was my fourth album to be certified **quadruple platinum**. I guess my fans liked it!

L ater that year, I launched another worldwide tour to promote *Red* and was on the road for almost two years. In 2013, I won a very special award from the Country Music Association. It's called the Pinnacle Award, and it's given to artists who have reached great levels of success. Garth Brooks is the only other singer to ever win it. It was a huge honor, and it meant so much that I cried when they gave it to me!

After headlining huge tours, releasing multiple albums, and winning some big awards, I was officially a star. One downside to being famous is that the media pays a lot of attention to me. I get photographed everywhere I go, and there are a lot of articles written about what I'm wearing or who I'm dating. It's nice that my fans want to know all about me, but sometimes people say things that are untrue or that really hurt my feelings. Mostly, I try to ignore those stories and focus on my music.

My fans are the best part of being a star. I love meeting them at shows and events. But my favorite thing is to totally surprise a fan. For example, I went to a prom with one fan for a show on MTV. One time, I took a car full of toys to a fan's home for her son after hearing she was having a hard time. I even photobombed a fan's family picture session in a Nashville park! Seeing the look on fans' faces when I surprise them is priceless. And getting to hear how my music has affected them means the world to me.

After four successful albums and three major tours, I decided it was time to change things up. I wrote a lot of new songs on the *Red* tour, and I realized that none of them were country songs. I was inspired by pop music and was ready to record my very first pop album! My record label wasn't sure if it was a good idea, but they trusted me. So I found the best pop songwriters and producers in the music industry and begged them to work with me. I spent most of 2014 writing, recording, and experimenting with my new sound—and it really paid off.

I released my fifth album, *1989*, in October 2014, and I was so nervous that I barely slept the night before it went on sale! I didn't have to be so worried, though, because my fans loved it. The album sold more than 1.2 million copies the first week it went on sale, making it my most successful release so far. Everyone embraced my new pop sound in songs like "Shake It Off" and "Blank Space." I am so glad that I trusted my instincts and tried something new. Fear should never hold you back from taking a risk!

T.S.   1989

I wanted my *1989* tour to be really special and different from my previous tours. I had lots of new fans who love pop music, and I even had a new band for the occasion. I'd been feeling inspired by Broadway shows, so I wanted my *1989* tour to have lots of big sets. I love surprising my audience whenever I can with special guests and new songs. I wanted this to be my best tour yet!

When *1989* came out, my career was going better than ever, but with that success and fame also came negative attention. There were more mean things said about me than ever before, especially on the internet, and it was hard for me to deal with hearing and reading all of it. Online bullies can be really cruel! I was feeling very low and decided to take some time for myself by moving to a new home and staying away from social media for a while.

While I was off social media, I spent time with family, friends, and loved ones, and I also worked on the music for my next album. I was inspired by electropop, R&B, and hip-hop, as well as the bullying and media scrutiny I'd dealt with, when I made my sixth album, *reputation*. Some of the songs, like "Look What You Made Me Do," were also inspired by the hit TV show *Game of Thrones*. It debuted at the top of the Billboard 200 and sold 1.2 million copies in its first week on sale in 2017. *Reputation* was also my last album with the Big Machine label.

On 2018, I went out on a stadium tour for *reputation*. The tour was so big, it broke records at the time! Netflix also released a **concert film** of the *reputation* tour. And that wasn't the only thing I was working on while on tour—the **documentary** *Miss Americana*, which came out on Netflix in January 2020, features footage from the *reputation* tour, too.

M iss *Americana* also shows me working on some of the songs and music videos for my seventh album, *Lover*, which came out in 2019. It was my first album released by Republic Records, and I wrote a lot of the songs about love, including love for my mother, who was sick when I wrote "Soon You'll Get Better." The whole album is really a love letter to love itself.

Around the same time *Lover* came out, the label I'd worked with on my first six albums was sold to a music manager who was a big bully. I'd been trying to buy my **master recordings** of those six albums back for years, and now they were owned and controlled by someone I did not get along with. I was mad and sad, and I started to form a plan: I would re-record my first six albums and release them all over again, with subtle changes to the old songs. I added new songs, too, so that I would own them once and for all.

In 2020, when the whole world was locked down during the COVID-19 pandemic, I used the time at home to keep working on new music. In July 2020 and December 2020, I released *folklore* and *evermore*, my eighth and ninth albums. I felt inspired by watching movies while I was at home, and I used my imagination to create characters and stories in the songs on *folklore*, like "Cardigan," "Betty," and "August." *Folklore* was my first surprise album, announced only a few hours before its release, and it was the bestselling album of 2020!

The success of *folklore* inspired me to keep imagining and playing with the same musical style, which led to the surprise release of *evermore* just a few months later. It felt really good to get creative in a new way, writing stories that weren't about my personal life into my songs. My time working on *evermore* overlapped with my re-recording of *Fearless*—I even recorded "Happiness" from *evermore* and "You Belong With Me (Taylor's Version)" from *Fearless (Taylor's Version)* on the same day!

FAVORITE POP ALBUM

TAYLOR SWIFT
"RED (TAYLOR'S VERSION)"

I released my first two re-recorded albums in 2021—*Fearless (Taylor's Version)* and *Red (Taylor's Version)*. Both re-recorded albums featured new songs, like "Message in a Bottle" on *Red (Taylor's Version)* and "Mr. Perfectly Fine" on *Fearless (Taylor's Version)*, plus new versions of the original songs, like a ten-minute version of "All Too Well" on *Red (Taylor's Version)*. They both sold more copies than the original versions of the albums did, so I guess people liked the new and updated songs a lot!

Then, in 2022, I released my tenth studio album, *Midnights*, as well as *Midnights (3am Edition)*, which had seven extra songs on it. *Midnights* was inspired by thirteen different times I had been up in the middle of the night. Sleep is important, but some great songs came out of those sleepless nights! The first single from *Midnights*, "Anti-Hero," was the top-selling song of 2022, and *Midnights* was the top-selling album of the year, too. And it won the Grammy for Album of the Year!

Because of the COVID-19 pandemic, I hadn't been on a tour for an album since 2018, and I'd released four brand-new albums, plus the new music on my re-recorded albums! So in 2023, I set out on the biggest and hardest world tour I've ever done: The Eras Tour. It was a **retrospective** tour of my whole career, featuring songs from at least nine of my ten albums. I started training six months before the first show. Each show lasted over two hours, and included more than forty songs, almost as many dance numbers, and sixteen costume changes. Whew!

It was worth all that work to put on a great show for my fans, especially since so many of them tried very hard to get tickets. I wanted to show my fans that I celebrate who I have been, who I am now, and who I will be—and that they should do the same for themselves. And they really showed up! The Eras Tour was the first music tour to earn over a billion dollars. I loved seeing my fans singing and dancing along, decked out in different Eras-themed outfits and trading friendship bracelets with my song lyrics on them.

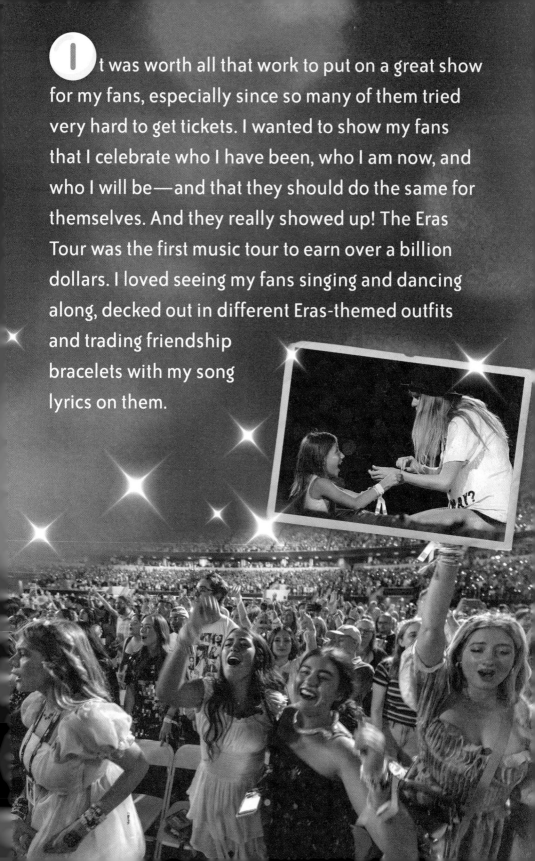

I had to build rest into my Eras Tour schedule, too, because those shows were hard and tiring. After performing a few shows in a row, I would rest for a full day. I only got out of bed to get food and then I would bring it back to bed and eat it there! It was fun to eat in bed and relaxing to rest all day, and it was really important for me to get that rest to be able to give it my all during such an intense show for so long.

On October 2023, I released a concert film of The Eras Tour in theaters. The movie theater chain AMC had its highest ticket sales in one day when *Taylor Swift: The Eras Tour* movie tickets went on sale, and Beyoncé came to the premiere, which was so cool! The movie brought the Eras show to fans who weren't able to come see it in person. In July and October 2023, I also released my next two re-recorded albums: *Speak Now (Taylor's Version)* and *1989 (Taylor's Version)*. I worked really, really hard in 2023!

y music career has given me the chance to do a lot of cool things other than music, too. I've launched two different clothing lines and designed greeting cards. I've been the face of a makeup line, and I was in a commercial with a ton of supercute kittens! I've released several of my own perfumes. I also appeared in concert movies for Miley Cyrus and the Jonas Brothers, as well as in music videos for my friends Brad Paisley and Kellie Pickler.

've also been able to try my hand at acting, which is so much fun! I've hosted *Saturday Night Live*, had **cameos** and roles in *New Girl*, *Valentine's Day*, *The Giver*, *Amsterdam*, and more. I played an animated character when I recorded the voice of Audrey in *The Lorax* and got to play one of my favorite animals—a cat!—in the 2019 film adaptation of the musical *Cats*. I've moved behind the camera, too, by directing some of my music videos, as well as the short film for the ten-minute version of "All Too Well."

It always feels great when other people love my music, and I feel honored each time I win a new award. So far, I've won fourteen Grammy Awards, forty American Music Awards, multiple Country Music Association Awards and Academy of Country Music Awards, forty Billboard Music Awards, twenty-three MTV Video Music Awards, and more, including a Primetime Emmy Award! Another way my work has been honored is that some college professors are teaching classes about my music! It's pretty cool to think of my lyrics being compared to classic poetry.

One of the biggest honors I've ever received came near the end of 2023, when *Time* magazine named me Person of the Year. I asked if I could bring my cat to the photoshoot (they said yes, so my cat was with me on the cover of *Time*!). I'm so grateful to *Time* for the honor, and to everyone who made my 2023 possible—especially my fans.

Another huge moment came during the 2024 Grammys. I won two awards, including Album of the Year! I was so grateful that I made a surprise announcement about the release of my next album, *The Tortured Poets Department*, which came out two months later, on April 19, 2024.

I've spent a lot of time on tour since my career started, and I'll likely go on more tours before my career is over. I've been lucky to have talented musicians tour with me, including Ed Sheeran, Florida Georgia Line, Neon Trees, Phoebe Bridgers, HAIM, Sabrina Carpenter, and more. My favorite thing about being on tour is getting to meet my fans in so many different places and hear their stories. I try to meet as many as I can—even if it means signing autographs for hours!

As much as I love being on the road, it's always nice to come home after a long trip. When I'm not working, I like to spend time with my friends, family, and my three cats, Meredith Grey, Olivia Benson, and Benjamin Button. Some of the things I love to do are cooking and baking (especially cakes and pancakes!), painting my nails, and crafting, like when my friends and I made homemade snow globes. My other passions include reading and hunting for antiques.

So, what's next for me? I plan to keep doing more of what I love: writing songs, recording music, touring, and working with other talented musicians. My job is better than I ever imagined it would be when I was a kid. I'm so thankful that I get to live out my dream by performing and making music every day, and I can't wait to see what the future will bring!

The lesson I've learned
the most often in life is
that you're always going to
know more in the future
than you know now.

—T.S.

(Taylor Swift)

TIME LINE

DECEMBER 13, 1989:
I was born in Reading, Pennsylvania.

2002:
I learned how to play guitar and wrote my very first song, "The Outside."

2006:
I signed a record deal with Big Machine Records and recorded and released my first album, *Taylor Swift*.

2010:
I released my third album, Speak Now, and had a small role in the movie *Valentine's Day*.

2012:
I released my fourth album, *Red*.

2000:
I started singing karaoke at fairs and festivals.

2003:
I moved to Nashville with my family to pursue my dream of becoming a country music star.

2008:
I released my second album, *Fearless*.

2011:
I traveled all over the world on my *Speak Now* tour and recorded the voice of Audrey in *The Lorax* animated movie.

2014:
I starred in the film *The Giver* and released my fifth album, *1989*.

2020:
folklore was released as my eighth studio album and my first surprise album, followed by *evermore*, my ninth album and second surprise album. I also started re-recording my first six albums.

2017:
I released my sixth album, and my last album with Big Machine, *reputation*.

2022:
Midnights, my tenth studio album, was released.

DECEMBER 2023:
I was named *Time* Person of the Year for 2023.

2019:
I released my seventh album, *Lover*, which was my first album released with my new label, Republic Records. I also acted in and wrote a song for the musical movie *Cats*.

2021:
Fearless (Taylor's Version) and *Red (Taylor's Version)* were released.

2023:
The Eras Tour kicked off in Glendale, Arizona. I released *Speak Now (Taylor's Version)*, *1989 (Taylor's Version)*, and *Taylor Swift: The Eras Tour* concert film.

FEBRUARY 2024:
After winning two Grammy Awards, I announced the release of my eleventh studio album, *The Tortured Poets Department*.

GLOSSARY

ALBUM: a long recording on a record, CD, or digital download that usually includes a set of songs

CAMEO: a small role in a movie, play, etc. that is performed by a well-known star

CONCERT FILM: a filmed version of a concert performance that is edited and released like a movie

DEMO TAPE: a recording that shows what a performer can do

DEVELOPMENT DEAL: when a music label promises to develop a musician's skills and image before committing to recording an album

DOCUMENTARY: a movie, TV, or radio program that uses real-life footage to provide a factual record of events

HEADLINING: being the main performer in a show or concert

KARAOKE: a form of entertainment in which people take turns singing popular songs into a microphone over pre-recorded music

MASTER RECORDING: the original recording of a song, sound, or performance

MUSIC LABEL: a company that produces musical recordings and represents musical artists and bands

PLATINUM: an award that is given to a singer or musical group for selling at least one million copies of a record

PRODUCER: someone who is in charge of making and usually providing the money for a play, movie, or record

QUADRUPLE PLATINUM: an award that is given to a singer or musical group for selling at least four million copies of a record

RECORD DEAL: a contract between a musician or band and a music label in which they agree to record and produce an album

RETROSPECTIVE: looking back on or dealing with past events or situations